Bedtime Stories for Stressed Out Adults: Relaxing Sleep Stories, Guided Mindfulness Meditations& Self-Hypnosis For Deep Sleep, Overcoming Anxiety, Insomnia & Stress Relief

By Meditation Made Effortless

Contents

1. Morning at the Seaside Cottage (60 Minutes) 2
2. Sheltering In The Book Store (50 Minutes)........8
3. The Night Train North (70 Minutes)..................14
4. The Sleepy Mountain (50 Minutes) 21
5. The Night Sky (50 Minutes) 26
6. A Walk Along the Canal (80 Minutes)..............32
7. A Walk Through The Magic Garden (60 Minutes) 40
8. Picnic Near the Waterfall (50 Minutes) 47
9. A Night On Your Paradise Island (70 Minutes) 53
10. A Trip Down the River (60 Minutes)..............60

© Copyright 2019 - All rights reserved.

The content contained within this book may not be reproduced, duplicated or transmitted without direct written permission from the author or the publisher.

Under no circumstances will any blame or legal responsibility be held against the publisher, or author, for any damages, reparation, or monetary loss due to the information contained within this book; either directly or indirectly.

Legal Notice:

This book is copyright protected. This book is only for personal use. You cannot amend, distribute, sell, use, quote or paraphrase any part, or the content within this book, without the consent of the author or publisher.

Disclaimer Notice:

Please note the information contained within this document is for educational and entertainment purposes only. All effort has been executed to present accurate, up to date, and reliable, complete information. No warranties of any kind are declared or implied. Readers acknowledge that the author is not engaging in the rendering of legal, financial, medical or professional advice.

1. Morning at the Seaside Cottage (60 Minutes)

Hello and welcome to this sleep story. Start by making yourself nice and comfortable in bed. Allow any thoughts or feeling from the day to drift away. Give your mind the chance to open itself up to the experience it's about to have. When you are ready, just allow your eyes to gently close. Fully experience how comfortable you feel under the covers. How nice it is to just spread out and have this time just for yourself. Sleep is a precious thing and should be treated as such. This is your time to relax and allow your mind and body to recharge for tomorrow.

Start by taking in a few deep breaths. And then allow the air to leave your body slowly. Do this a few times until you can feel the relaxing benefits. Then just allow yourself to breath naturally as you start your journey to the seaside cottage.

There is a beautiful cottage by the sea. It's right on the edge of the beach, giving the occupier an amazing view of the sea and the distant horizon. The cottage is old but still looks warm and inviting. You can tell that it has been home to families who have grown up there and who have appreciated everything that the cottage has to offer. Just by being here for a day, you can make yourself feel so much more relaxed and happy. So carefree and without any worries.

This is an amazing place to come to after you have spent the day at the beach. After taking in the beautiful sun beaming down on you, there is nothing better than heading to the seaside cottage, getting warm underneath a blanket and sitting by a nice log fire. Then you could sit on the porch and look up at the amazing night sky. It's incredible how when you're in a place like this, undisturbed by artificial lights of any kind, that you can see just how amazing the sky at night can be. How you can just gaze up for hours on end and allow your mind to drift off, thinking about what might be out there. About the new worlds you could be gazing at.

While the night's at the seaside cottage are amazing, nothing really can compare with the early mornings. If you are awake for sunrise, you can watch the beautiful morning sun slowly rising over the sea. Many people like to make themselves a nice cup of coffee and then sit on the deck and just watch the sun rise. Watch the orange colour spread over the sea in the distance until you can see the top of the sun poking out over the gentle waves. And then just watch as it continues to rise. And you can hear the seagulls greeting it good morning as it rises.

It always feels so comfortable on the cottage deck first thing in the morning. Even though it is a lot cooler than it can be during the day, it still feels a comfortable temperature. A nice steady breeze comes up from the sea and you can hear the gentle waves flowing over the sand. You can see the seagulls flying around, getting ready for all the visitors that will be coming to the beach in the hopes that they can get hold of some leftover picnic food.

The waves always seem so much calmer in the morning. You can walk along the beach in bare feet and allow the water to wash over you. The water will come up to the top of your ankle sometimes but the strength of the waves never feel like they could cause you problems. Instead you can stand there and allow the water to gently wash over you. The sea water can feel so cool and calming. If it has been a particularly warm night in the cottage, this can be amazing way to cool down a little. To just stand there, close your eyes, and fully the experience the sensations that the sea water brings as it washes over your feet. How you can feel the water weaving through your toes. How you can hear the waves around you and how they sound so much louder than they feel. You could just stand there for hours. Just feeling the rising sun becoming warmer and warmer against your skin.

You can then go for a walk along the beach near the cottage as the sun continues to rise. And when you do, you can take a moment to think about the magic of this place and what it means to you. This place is so wonderful and calming that all the troubles and struggles of life can simply wash away. It can almost feel like all the things that have been making you feel stressed or anxious have been carried away by the sea water and it flowed over your feet. This is an amazing place and it is here just for you. This is somewhere where you can truly let go and allow yourself to have a moment of peace and quiet. A place where you can totally relax and allow all of those life worries to drift away to sea. Until you can no longer see them in the distant horizon.

If on the walk back to the cottage you are coming from the south side, you can truly see what a magnificent little building it is. You can see it's made of wood but you know it has to be strong wood. This cottage has been here for so long. It has withstood the blasts of storms and sand battering the sides. It has managed to hold off all of that for so long. It's no wonder then that when you step inside after coming back from a walk, you can feel so perfectly safe.

After going for a walk and standing in the sea, it always feels nice to have a warm shower. Just to allow all of the sand and the salt crystals left behind by the sea to wash off your body. When you step out of the shower you feel so warm and comfortable. Then you can make yourself another cup of coffee and go back out onto the deck.

It's always amazing to sit on the porch during the early mornings at the seaside cottage. Just to sit there with a book and a coffee and just allowing yourself to have some time to yourself. In the modern world, it can always feel like you can't have moments of peace. Even when you are by yourself, you could still be receiving messages on your phone about work or something that is demanding your attention. But here, at the seaside cottage, nothing needs your attention. This is a place where you can truly relax and not worry about having to do anything.

You can just sit back, drink your coffee and read your book as you feel the sun rising. And even though you have had two cups of coffee, you still could allow yourself to drift off for a morning sleep. That's how relaxing this place can be. That's how much mental and physical freedom you can have in this place.

After reading a few chapters of your book, you put it down on the small table beside you. You finish the last of your coffee and then you lean back in your chair. Then, you just allow your eyes to gently close.

You enjoy the feeling of the morning sun caressing your skin. You enjoy the sound of the seagulls in the distance. You enjoy the sound of the gentle waves as they crash against the sand. You fully appreciate how this wonderful serenity feels. And with that in mind, you are now able to just allow yourself to drift off to sleep, fully appreciating the amazing feeling you get simply by sitting on the porch of the seaside cottage.

2. Sheltering In The Book Store (50 Minutes)

Hello and welcome to tonight's sleep story. Tonight, we are going to be taking a trip to the book store. But before we can begin perusing the shelves looking for the next novel to read, we need to make ourselves nice and comfortable. So, climb into bed and make yourself feel warm and comfortable under the covers. Allow your head to be held by place by gravity on the pillow. Take in some deep breaths and then slowly breathe out. Do this a few times until you notice that the tension you might have been holding in your body has started to drift away. When you feel nice and comfortable, just allow yourself to breathe naturally. Now that you are ready, we can start out story.

If you have ever been caught in a downpour whilst walking down the street, you will know what a relief it is is to find a shop that is inviting enough to allow you to shelter. This book store we are about to enter is just one such place. At the moment, it is raining heavily and you are running down the street with your jacket held over your head to try and protect yourself. It's only been raining for a matter of seconds and already you know that you are going to be drenched by this downpour if you don't get shelter soon. This is when you notice the book shop just at the bottom of the road., You run down as quick as you can, obviously making sure that you don't slip along the way. And then you dart inside the shop and shut the door behind you.

As you walked in, you noticed the large windows the shop has facing out into the street. In the windows there are a wide range of books, from recent releases to some of the year's best sellers. The windows also display some of the finest old books, some of which could tell whole stories just by looking at their worn and battered covers.

This book shop is always open late. Which is lucky as the sun is now starting to set and the night is starting to close in. This doesn't effect the rain however, which continues to hammer down. You can hear the rain clattering against the large windows. The clattering becomes louder even now and then when the wind picks up a little.

Outside, you see the street lamps are starting to come on. They cast an orange light down on the wet pavement outside. The street lamp just outside the shop comes on now and illuminates in the books in the window, almost like they now have their own personal spotlight.

Above your head, you notice that the shop has a skylight as well. You look at it for a moment and watch the rain clattering against it. It's satisfying to watch the rain coming down, knowing that none of the rain will be able to make you uncomfortable and wet. You listen to the sound of the rain becoming heavier as the rain drops begin to mix with hail. You get the feeling you might be in here for a while, but you feel okay about that. There are certainly much worse places to be stuck during a heavy rain fall.

Just in the corner, you spot a comfortable looking leather chair. You can imagine that when people are visiting this store, they will frequently take a book they find interesting from the shelf and then sit down and enjoy flicking through it in comfort for a moment. You can imagine yourself taking an armful of books from the shelves and just sitting their and flicking through them for hours on end.

Next to the chair is a table on wheels and a sign that says you can leave any books that you have picked up there. You like this feature as it means you don't have to painstakingly remember where every single book you have picked up belongs. But then you think that if you owned this shop, this feature would be for you just as much as it is for the customers. If the owner of the shop is anything like you, then they would relish the thought of being able to walk around this shop with the trolley of books, finding where to put them back on the shelf. What a wonderful opportunity it would be to reacquaint yourself with all the knowledge and the stories that are available under this one roof.

In the other corner of the room, you can see Peter, the owner of the store. Peter is known in this area as being one of the nicest people you could ever meet. Always impeccably dressed in a suit with a waistcoat, you will always find him sat in the corner by his desk, reading one of the many books that have been dropped off with him for donations. It is said that Peter has read every single book that has ever been in that shop and the amount of knowledge he has gathered over the years could fill three libraries.

As always with customers, Peter greets you with a smile and tells you to have a look around and take your time. He says that you should make yourself comfortable so then you don't have to brave the rain until it calms. You thank him and take the opportunity to have a look over the shelves.

It's surprising because this doesn't seem like a large book shop, but it feels like every subject is represented here. As you pass the history section, you can see all the different subsections labelled perfectly. Victorian history. Tudor history. Chinese history. Even Icelandic history. You decide that you would like to sit down and have a look through some of these books. You take three or four from the shelf and then move over to the chair in the corner.

As you sit down, you fully appreciate the support that the chair is giving you. Even though you have only just sat down, you already feel incredibly comfortable and relaxed. It feels like the chair was designed exclusively to support your body. You get nice and comfortable and pick up the first book.

As you pick up the book, you look up to the skylight again and watch the continuing rain and hail. For you, this downpour could last all night. It would not matter to you one bit. You can't think of anywhere else you would like to be sheltering from the rain.

Just as you sink in the chair a little more, Peter walks over with a hot cup of tea. He places it on the table next to you and says that he figured you would need that to warm yourself up after being caught in that rain. You thank him and he tells you to take your time and enjoy the selection of books you have chosen. He says he has read them and would recommend all of them.

Peter smiles and then walks back over to his desk and continues reading his book. You take a sip from the tea he has given you. Even that first sip feels so comforting and warming. You can feel the effects drifting through your body. Any signs of tension or discomfort in your body now slowly floating away.

You sink a little deeper into the seat and pick up that first book again and start reading. And then, as you turn the book over to the next page, you find yourself slowly drifting off. Just gradually falling asleep now as you read. You take another sip of tea and feel the warmth and calming effects flowing through you. And then you gently close your eyes and drift off. And as you do, all you can hear is the sound of the rain and hail clattering down on the skylight above you.

3. The Night Train North (70 Minutes)

Welcome to tonight's sleep story. Tonight, we are going to be taking the night train to the north. So before we begin, making sure that you are nice and comfortable in bed. Get settled under the covers and get into a comfortable position. Then when you are ready, gently close your eyes. Allow any thoughts you might be having to drift away. Enjoy the feeling of having a calm mind. There is nothing that you need to think about right now. All you have to do is get comfortable and relax. Take in a deep breath and then release the air slowly. Do this a couple more times. Enjoy how doing this makes you feel. When you start to feel more comfortable, just allow your breathing to return to its natural rhythm.

Are you ready? Good. Then we will begin our story.

The sun has just started to set as you take your seat on that night train. You look out of the window and you can see the sun gently starting to set. It's just starting to disappear behind the station where the last few passengers are waiting for the next train. You hear the wheels starting to whir into motion as you slowly start to be carried away from the station. You watch the scenery around you as your train starts to pick up more speed. The station where you started is already starting to disappear into the distance. As you take in your surroundings, you can hear the gentle sound of the engine working. Speeding up the train more and more as you gently start to move forwards. Just a gentle forward motion slowly taking you down the tracks.

As you look out of the window, you can see the grassy hills and the distant river. You can see the sunset being reflected in the calm water as the sun continues to set. The only thing that can distract you from this view is the occasional glistening of the lights on the track, curling in the distance. You can see all the yellows and the reds of the shining lights. You're gradually heading towards them and they look inviting.

As the train moves through the hills, a rainfall starts. It's very gentle. You can hear the rain tapping gently on the roof of the train. It's a soothing sound. In the distance, you can see the drops of water gently landing on the distant river. You watch the drops hitting the water. How the sound of the rain hitting the roof of the train almost matches the rhythm of the rain hitting the river. It sounds almost like you are listening to a gentle song. Like you are being serenaded on your journey.

Your seat on the train is comfortable. It has a tall back and plenty of legroom so you can stretch out and relax. You have a table in front of you and there is a little sign saying that you can connect to the wi-fi if you wish. But you don't want to. All you want to do is fully take in this moment and the feelings that you have on this journey.

You look around. You take in the surroundings on the train and what you can see outside. You notice the rain picking up and the small drops of water hitting the window next to you. You watch the small beads of water as they start to move down the glass. Then as the train picks up a little more speed, you notice the little drops moving to the side as well. Struggling to cling to the glass as the wind and the speed of the train try and blow the beads of rain away. You watch this happening as you settle a little more into your seat. It feels so comfortable and warm.

You're moving through beautiful fields now. Every blade of grass looks vibrantly green and inviting. You enjoy feeling like you are far from civilization now. Almost like this train journey is just for you and you alone. You notice that the rain clouds are now starting to move over the night sky as the sun continues to disappear over the horizon.

As you watch the sun slowly disappearing, you can see a herd of cows grazing in the field far in the distance. There aren't any human beings around. You look and you can't see any other people for miles around. It feels like you have found a quiet corner of the world just for yourself. Like you have created a special place where you can be free of your stresses and anxieties. Where you can be free of anything that has been on your mind for a while. You enjoy the feeling of having a clear mind as you watch the cows. The fields. The gentle rainfall against the window.

You look out of the opposite window and all you can see is the open ocean. In the distance, you can see some big fishing vessels, coming back in to shore with their catches from the day. Even though the train is moving fast and in the opposite direction to the vessels, it still looks like they are gently floating away at a slow pace. It takes several minutes before they disappear out of view of the window.

As you look at the ocean, you notice how smooth it looks. It's almost like it's reacting to the setting sun and is settling down for a comfortable night. As you look at this, a gentle voice comes over the tannoy and announces that you will soon be arriving at the first station on your route. The station stands out against the picturesque surroundings and doesn't seem to have any connection to a town or a city. It's strange seeing a station like this in the middle of nowhere. Perhaps it is not surprising then that when the train comes to a stop at the station, you can only see two people getting onto the train. They both run frantically, hoping they will not get too wet moving onto the train from under the small roof covering the tiny platform.

The station is made almost entirely of wood that has been painted red. A large clock hangs from the front of the station, making sure that no passengers are ever stuck for the current time. You look into the waiting room, illuminated by the two or three ceiling lights. You imagine that if the train wasn't here, chances are the light in that waiting room would be the only light around for miles. You imagine being able to see it all the way back at the calm river that you passed a while ago.

As you look at the waiting room, you see a women in a raincoat. She's reading a book she's holding in one hand while cradling a cup of hot coffee in the other. You can see the steam rising from the cup. She takes a sip and you can see that it's comforting her and making her feel a little warmer. Given how late it is getting, you know that this woman must be preparing herself for a long journey if she's having coffee at this hour. Perhaps even longer than the journey you're on now. You have no doubt that she will be looking forward to her trip just as much as you have been looking forward to yours. You get the feeling that all she will need is her book and perhaps another cup of coffee to keep her warm as she watches the scenery go by. And perhaps watches the rain hitting the window next to her. You watch her turn from her book as she watches the last bit of the sun disappear over the horizon before settling down to her book once again.

Your train starts to rhythmically move again. One of the new passengers walks through your carriage. They look at you and smile and nod. You smile and nod back at them as they walk past you. A beverage carriage comes down the aisle and inspired by the man you saw, you ask for a cup of tea. The person serving you smiles as they fill a cup with hot, steamy water. They remove the tea bag and add a little milk. They then put it down on the table in front of you with a smile and say that they hope you will enjoy your night on the train.

You notice the comfortable blanket that you have by your side. You take a sip of tea and enjoy the feeling of the hot liquid as it moves from your throat through your body. It's a nice comfortable feeling. You can feel any tension that you have been holding slowly starting to drift away. This train journey is exactly what you need. Making you feel so comfortable and relaxed. So free of stress and anxiety. So comfortable.

You take the blanket and start wrapping yourself up in it. Then you take another sip of tea. You feel the relaxation and the warmth moving through your arms and legs. All of your muscles relaxing and becoming more and more comfortable. Any tension that you might be holding in your neck or your back or your shoulders just drifting away,

The gentle voice over the tannoy announces the next stop, but you are not able to focus on it. It just drifts through your mind like nothing has happened. You are too comfortable now. Too relaxed. All that matters is how comfortable you feel. You take another sip of the warming tea before you settle under the blanket. You gently close your eyes and start to drift off to sleep. All you can hear as you drift off is the gentle sound of the engine and the tapping of the rain on the train roof.

4. The Sleepy Mountain (50 Minutes)

Good evening. Welcome to tonight's story. Tonight, we are going to be spending the night on the top of the sleepy mountain. One of the most relaxing places on earth. Before we begin, make sure that you are nice and comfortable. Get under the cover and close your eyes. Get into a nice comfortable position and allow any thoughts you may be having to drift away slowly. Nothing needs your attention right now. Just allow all your thoughts to come to a natural conclusion. And then bring your awareness to your breathing as you take in a deep breath and then exhale slowly. Do this a couple more times and then allow yourself to breathe normally.

Are you comfortable? Perfect. Now let's start our journey.

As you watch night drift in on the sleepy mountain, you think about how you have never seen anything so beautiful. The sky turns dark blue within seconds and it moves over you, almost like a thick blanket. It's like the world is being tucked into bed under a comfortable duvet for the night. As soon as the sky turns dark blue, you hear the birds starting to settle down for a good night's sleep. Soon their chorus ends and instead it is replaced with the sounds of crickets and the occasional hooting of a distant owl.

As you watch the sun disappear in the distant, casing one final shadow through the trees before calling it a day, you can see why this mountain is referred to as the sleepy mountain. You get the feeling that in the natural world, there are few places as comfortable and inviting as this. Few places that can make you feel so comfortable. Not just with your surroundings, but in your own skin as well. Just by looking at this place, you know that stress or feelings of anxiety do not belong here. This is a place of peace and happiness. That is why you find it so easy to just let those feelings of stress to just float away, almost like they have been caught in the mountain breeze.

When you are here on the mountain, it can feel like the whole world has gone quiet. It's almost like a quiet is descending on the whole world out of respect for what is here. The nature and sheer relaxing spirit of this place make it wonderfully unique. It is here that people often come to find serenity and peace.

Too much of our lives is dictated by work and the stresses and anxieties that come from living in the modern world. When you think of all the things that demand our attention all of the time, it's no surprising that people often find themselves overcome with feelings of stress and then develop a strong desire to take a break from it all. This sleepy mountain is the perfect place to do just that.

Here, there is no place for stress and anxiety. It would not fit into this place. That is why, as soon as you set foot on this beautiful landscape, all of those feelings simply drift away. They stop being a part of you. Instead, the mountain becomes part of you. It becomes a symbol of your happiness and how peaceful you feel in this moment.

You can see the very faint sight of car headlights in the far distance. They are coming from the road near the river down below the mountain. Even though you can see them, you cannot hear them. Normally, you would be able to hear the gentle hum of the traffic. Here, it's almost like even the cars on the road know not to disturb this place.

Even though this place is quiet, it is by no means silent. You can still hear the birds in the trees all trying to get the last word before they settle down to sleep. You can still hear the distant sound of crickets that are coming out to dance in the moonlight. The owl is still occasionally hooting in the distance. And you can hear the sound of the gentle breeze flowing through the tree branches near you. The trees sway gently in reaction to the wind, but the breeze is so gentle, it is a slight movement. The breeze is comforting against your skin. It's almost like the mountain is giving you a gift to try and help you become more relaxed. And every now and then, you can hear the sound of other night animals awakening from their day's rest.

You are sat on the deck of a beautiful log cabin. It is situated in a prime spot for you to have a glorious view over the entire mountainside. It's a magical place. Just the view alone is enough to make you feel comfortable and relaxed in your surroundings. As you look up, you can see the stars are slowly starting to appear. In the distance, where you can see a small collection of houses not far from the lake and the road, you can see some of the lights starting to come on. They shine like yellow and orange stars in the distance.

You sit back and fully take in how amazing this place is. It feels like time is almost slowing down. There is no need to rush or live life at the speed you might find in a city or bustling town. Instead, everything here goes at a calm and comfortable pace. No need to rush. No need to feel stress. All you have to do is sit back, relax and enjoy the experience of simply being here.

As you sit back on your wooden chair outside your log cabin, you can feel yourself becoming more tired. More sleepy. It's now that you know what this mountain is referred to as sleepy mountain. It is the best place in the world to simply curl up and have a peaceful night's sleep. It's like the sounds of the wind and the owls are almost serenading you as you slowly start to drift off.

This is the perfect place to come and rest after a busy day. If you ever find yourself having a stressful day where you are running around trying to deal with all the things that are demanding your attention, then I highly recommend that you end that day with a visit to the sleepy mountain. It's here that you will be able to put all of those things aside and simply enjoy having the time to yourself. A time where you can allow your mind and body to fully rest and recharge. You will be surprised just how positive an effect this place can have on you. If you visit here enough at night, you will find that you sleep comfortably through the night. And you will find that you are better equipped to deal with those stresses in life when the day comes calling.

5. The Night Sky (50 Minutes)

Hello and welcome to tonight's sleep story. As night falls, you will enter a state of rest and tranquillity as we spend some time enjoying the beauty of the night sky. So, before we begin, make yourself as comfortable as possible. Get nice and cosy under the duvet and allow the bed to support the weight of your body. Enjoy the feeling of allowing your head to rest comfortably on your pillow. And then, when you feel ready, close your eyes. Stretch out into a position where you feel like you could fall asleep.

Now turn your attention to your breathing for a moment. Take in a nice deep breath. Hold it inside for a moment and then slowly exhale. Notice how the tension is leaving your body as the air leaves. Do this a few more times, then just allow yourself to breathe normally. Allow any thoughts you may be having to come to an end. Just give your mind the space to experience clarity and stillness. Now that we are ready, we can begin our story.

It's the beginning of Summer and the evening is drawing in. It's one of those early days of summer where it still feels warm but the sun is still setting at an earlier time that it would be at the height of the season. You step out of your home and allow your front door to gently close behind you. You feel the nice gentle breeze caressing your face as soon as you step outside. It feels nice and comforting. As you start to walk, you get to fully experience how comfortable the air feels tonight. Because it is early in the Summer season, it doesn't yet feel overwhelmingly hot. The air has a nice comfortable temperature which makes walking at a steady pace feel good.

After walking for a moment, you pause and take a little moment to enjoy the feeling of being outside at this time. The streets around you are nice and quiet. It would feel like you were all alone if it wasn't for the yellow and orange glows of the windows along the street. These are the only indicators that anyone is even around. For all you know, you are the only person in the world at this moment. Just you and the gentle breeze flowing around you.

As you continue walking to the end of your street, you walk past the small garden feature at the end of your road. It's filled with daffodils and roses. It's incredible how quickly this small garden has grown over the last few months. Almost like it's had a growth spurt in excitement of what summer will bring. The plants flow gently in the breeze as you walk past. You then look at the town houses around you. Along with the yellow and orange lights streaming from the windows, you can see the occasional shadow of people settling down for the night. Enjoying the peaceful nature of the night and of the summer breeze.

As you come to the end of your street, you make a turn and start walking up the hill. Within a few minutes of walking up the cobbled road, you already feel like you're in a completely different place. You turn and look back and see all the town houses. All still emitting their orange and yellow lights. You are going somewhere where you will not be able to see those lights. The only light you will be able to see are the ones being beamed down from the night sky by the moon and the stars.

The cobbled road is steep but not too steep that's difficult to walk along. Within a few minutes you are surrounded by beautiful trees and lush vegetation. You suddenly feel so surrounded by life. In the distance, you can hear the sound of birds singing as they settle down for a good night's rest. Every now and then, you can also hear an owl hooting as it gets ready to fully experience the night.

As you reach the end of the road, you move into the trees and start following the worn, brown path that has been forged in the ground. It guides you through the trees and out into a clearing. Here the grass is nice and short and shimmering gently in the breeze. As you walk into the clearing you look up to the night sky. It's amazing how different it looks here than it did outside your home. From your door, you could see the occasional spot of light being forced through the artificial light around you. Here, there is no artificial light to disturb your view. Now you can see a huge array of stars. Just slightly to the left is the moon, shining down on your like a silver spotlight.

You sit down on the grass and continue to look up at the sky. As you take it all in, time just seems to slow down. There is nowhere else you need to be. Nothing that needs your attention in this moment. All you need to do is sit and relax and look at the amazing view of the universe you have before you. There is such an amazing array of colours coming from the stars. Some are a darker blue or a sky blue. Others are yellow and even a couple that are red. You wonder which ones are the planets in the solar system and wonder if the slightly larger, flickering red light is the sunlight bouncing off the surface of Mars.

You feel amazing during this moment. You feel so calm and at peace with yourself and your surroundings. This clearing in the middle of this field is almost like your own personal paradise. Here, there is no need to worry about things or waste your mental energy on things that might cause you stress and anxiety. All you have to do right now is sit back and fully enjoy this amazing moment.

This time is just for you and you alone. There is no one else in this clearing. Everyone else is at home settling down for that. You have this space totally for yourself to sit and look at the stars and dream about what might be out there. About the new worlds shining their warm light down on you.

You lie back on the grass. You spread your arms and legs out wide so you can get completely comfortable. It hasn't rained for a few days now so the grass feels dry and comfortable. Enjoy the feeling of being held in this place by gravity, while about you, the universe keeps rotating and expanding. All those stars looking down on you all have their own stories to tell. About how they were born millions of years ago and how they have planets circling them just like our solar system. You wonder what those planets are like. Whether they are hot or cold. Big or small. Made of gas or rock. Just allowing yourself to dream of what might be out there.

You take another look at the moon and enjoy the feeling of being able to see it shine so brightly in the sky. You can almost make out all the little details on the moon's surface. And as you are looking at it, you just slowly allow your eyes to close. You feel the wonderful breeze flowing past you. You hear the sound of the distant owl hooting as it heads out into the trees for the night. And as you are listening, you slowly allow yourself to drift to sleep. Your mind filled with wonderful, calming thoughts about all those new worlds that could be waiting for you out there in the universe.

6. A Walk Along the Canal (80 Minutes)

Good evening. Tonight, we are going to take a lovely stroll along the canal. But before we begin, make sure that you are nice and comfortable. Take a moment to get settled under the covers in a comfortable position. Then close your eyes and allow any thoughts you may be having to drift away. Enjoy the feeling of being comfortable and feeling safe and secure. Take in a few deep breaths and allow the tension to leave your body as you exhale. Enjoy this feeling. Notice how you are sinking deeper and deeper into the bed.

Are you ready? Perfect. Now we can start our walk.

The canal looks beautiful today. It's almost completely still and looks like a silky, crystal blanket. You imagine that when it is a particularly hot summer day, it would be nice to take a dip in this canal and just allow the blanket of water to wash over you. Making you feel completely comfortable and one with nature.

The water along the canal is so still it looks like glass. As you look at it, you can see the reflection of the gently moving trees behind you and on the opposite side. You take in a deep breath and enjoy the cool crispness of the air. It makes your airways feel so clear. No pollution from cars here. Just the wonderful crisp air. When you breathe out, you can almost feel the air carrying away the feelings of tension or stress you have been carrying. Just by appreciating the air by the canal, you are already feeling more comfortable and relaxed. You know that this canal is not the sort of place where you want to be carrying stress or anxiety. That's why you let it go without putting up any fight at all. Just allowing those feelings to drift away in the gentle breeze.

As you start walking, you see a tiny group of ducks making their way along the water near the opposite embankment. Up until now, it has been like you were the only living thing around. Seeing them calmly going about their day reminds you how teaming with life this area will be. How for those ducks, this blissful place is somewhere they get to call home. You watch the effects the ducks have on the water as they swim. Creating tiny ripples that move out into the canal as they get wider until they fade away.

You continue watching the ducks as they swim further and further away. Soon the only way you know they have been there is because of the remaining ripples they have left behind them on the surface of the water. On the glass-like surface, it's the only thing that has disturbed these waters. And after a moment, they go completely still again. Almost like they it has suddenly frozen in a quick frost.

As you continue to walk, you walk past an old fishing boat. Even though it has clearly been through a lot in its life, it still looks warm and inviting. You imagine what it must be like to take that boat out onto these calm waters. To just sit and fish for hours on end, just drinking tea and enjoying the calmness of the moment. You wonder if there are many fish in this canal and then you think that maybe that's not the point. Maybe just having a place where you can be totally at peace with yourself and your surroundings is all you need when you're on this boat.

The canal is so long, it seems to stretch into the horizon forever. You have only come here for a quick stroll, but the length of the canal does not bother you. If anything, you feel so relaxed that you feel like you could walk along it for hours on end. If you were still here as night drew in you would be happy. The scenery and the stillness of the canal makes you feel like you could stay here forever. You can imagine yourself walking laps of the canal for a long time. You could even see yourself just sitting on a canal boat and watching the reflections in the water. Just you and a flask of tea, watching the relexation of the sun slowly being replaced with a reflection of the moon.

When you think about the fast paced nature of life at the moment, you wonder why more people do not come to places like this. The unrelenting nature of technology and work means that many people feel like they never have a moment to switch off. Never have a moment to simply focus on being alive. And yet, you know now that places like this are exactly what you need. In this place, time is slowing down and this does not worry you. You don't feel like you have to be somewhere else or you should be thinking about other things. All you are thinking about is how beautiful this canal is and how it is helping you connect with nature. Connect with the world.

You know that you have no need to rush. There is nowhere you need to be. Nothing that needs your attention right now. If anything, you have a desire to walk a little slower along the canal. Just to give your mind and body the chance to fully embrace this experience. A chance to fully enjoy your surroundings. You know that you have all the time you need to simply breathe this all in. Just to allow any feelings of tension or stress to wash away. Almost like the ripples that you saw on the canal water surface.

There is little to no noise around you. Every now and then, you can hear the gentle ripple of the water, but even this is a faint sound. When the grass on the opposite side of you becomes long, you can hear the occasional stick insect singing. Almost like it is saying hello to you as you walk past. At this canal, you are just far enough away from civilization that you can't hear the gentle humming of cars on the road. Normally, you would be able to hear that sound in most places. But that sound doesn't belong in a place like this.

As you're walking, you notice that there is a small pub in the distance. It's on the other side of the canal and it looks warm and inviting. It has comfortable seating outside so you can sit and face the canal. You decide that you will stop there once you reach it and have a nice, cold drink. A nice chance to rest your legs for a moment and to just be still and enjoy the surroundings.

You wonder how many people must visit that pub each day. Then again, you imagine that it's quiet atmosphere and the sense of solitude that it gives you is rather the point of its existence. The landlord may well be quite happy to only have steady footfall if it means that both he and his customers get a chance to just be still and enjoy a refreshing drink in the midday sun.

As much as you are looking forward to going in the pub, you know that there is no need to rush. In this place, there is no need to hurry at all. Time has no meaning in this place. There is no need for urgency. You know that you will get to the pub eventually. But in the meantime, you can simply enjoy keep walking. Just walking and enjoying everything that the scenery has to offer.

Every now and then, you notice small birds flying around the canal. Some of them drop down to eat at small patches of moss, or attempt to dig out worms from the dusty ground. A few of them even fly and land quite close to you. They have no reason to be scared of you or your presence.

You are exuding such a calm and relaxed aura that these birds know that you will only appreciate their presence. Much like the stick insects you have passed, some of the chirp at you in a greeting as you walk past them. You smile at them in response and they look at you almost like they have registered your good nature.

As you approach the pub, you notice yet another group of ducks is making its was down the canal. You stop and watch them for a moment. You wonder if they are joining the group that you saw earlier. The swim close to the opposite side of the canal. They pass underneath the hanging trees, giving them some brief moments of shade from the sun beating down on them. They slow down as they pass under the branches, almost taking the opportunity to get as much of the shade as they can. They seem like they are almost savouring the moment.

As you watch them, you know that they don't consider the sun to be unpleasant. In fact, when they are passed the branches and they are exposed to the sunlight again, they seem quite happy to be back under the warm rays. It's simply that they are enjoying the experience of being on the canal. They like the shade just as much as they like the sunlight. Much like yourself, they simply want to take a moment and appreciate everything that this canal has to offer. They are completely free of any concerns. They can simply drift down the canal slowly and enjoy the feeling of calmness that surrounds them.

You reach the pub. You order yourself a large drink with ice and then you take a seat on one of the benches outside. You stretch your feet out and take a sip of your drink. The coolness of it fills your body, making you feel completely relaxed. You look out over the canal and then gently close your eyes. As you do, all you can hear is the sound of the canal moving gently and the birds chirping in the distance.

You take another sip of your drink now as the coolness spread around your body once more. And then, you quietly drift off, just listening to the sound of the birds and then gentle canal.

7. A Walk Through The Magic Garden (60 Minutes)

Hello and welcome to tonight's sleep story, where we will be making a visit to the Magic Garden. Before we begin, take a moment to make yourself feel nice and comfortable. Get settled under the covers and get into a position where you feel like you could fall asleep. Then when you are ready, just gently allow your eyes to close. Enjoy how it feels to shut the world out for the day. Take in some nice deep breaths and then allow the air to slowly leave your body. Enjoy the feeling of tension leaving your body. Once you feel nice and comfortable, just allow yourself to breathe normally. Now that you are comfortable, we will begin our story.

Our story begins as the sun rises over what the local villagers call the Magic Garden. As the sun rises over the stone walls that surround the edges of the garden, the warmth of the light hits the plants. They almost react in the light, like they are stretching out to start the new day. As the sun rises further, it hits the small bushes and bounces off the surface of the pond and the water in the fountain at the centre of the garden.

Tonight's story is all about Peter. Peter is the main who tends to the Magic Garden. This is something he has done since he was 18. Before that, he would help his father take care of the garden. His father had actually created the garden when he was 18 and had been taking care of it every since. Every day he would go and deal with the weeds and feed the fish in the fish pond. Peter would go with his father almost every morning from the point he turned six. He would get up extra early to go with him so he could help with the garden before school. It was his father's pride and joy. Now, it's Peter's pride and joy.

Peter has learned everything about gardening from his father. How to remove weeds without damaging the plants. What to do when foxes are disturbing the hedging. Whenever Peter needs to add new plants to the garden, he always thinks about how his dad would search for hours to find the right one. Every living thing in the garden had to be perfect.

Peter left early just like he did every morning. He closed the door of his cottage and then headed to the garden. Peter always preferred getting to the garden nice and early so then he could tend to the plants before more people arrived. Nearly every morning while walking to the garden, he would think about walking with his dad. Holding his hand as he walked and feeling so excited to get to the garden so he could start work. He would often ask his dad if the garden was actually magical. His father told him that it is magical if he believes it is. Since then, Peter has always believed deep down that it is indeed magical.

When Peter arrived that morning, he started by sweeping away the stay leaves that had blown over the cobbled paths during the night. Luckily it had been a relatively calm Spring night, so he didn't have to spend too long clearing them away. He then started filling the bird feeders in the trees, which were now starting to attract a wide array of birds. A blue tit sat on a branch nearby watching him as he filled one of the feeders. He smiled at the bird as he finished and beckoned it over. The blue tit cautiously approached and then started eating gleefully as Peter walked away.

Peter fished the leaves out of the fountain with a net. As he cleared away the few leaves that had blown in overnight, he looked at all the coins resting at the bottom of the fountain. All the wishes that had been made by children and parents. He felt like there was more coins than usual. It made him wonder if there was something in the air recently that was making people hope their wishes would come true. And he wondered if those people did truly believe the garden was magical, for he knew that if they truly believed then what they wished for would come true.

Peter watched the beautiful fountain for a moment, taking in the majesty of the falling water. Then he turned his attention to the fish pond. He ran his net over the top and removed the leaves from the surface. As he did, the fish in the pond rose to the surface, hoping that Peter has not forgotten their early morning meal. Peter reached into his bag and pulled out the fish food. The fish almost seemed to react in excitement at the sight of the bag. Peter reaches into it and pulls out a handful of food. He scatters it over the surface of the pond and the fish rush to get their breakfast. Peter watches them as they hoover up the food in short order. He feels a momentary temptation to give them more, but he knows he should not over feed them. Instead he leaves them and turns his attention back to the rest of the garden.

Peter always enjoys how the garden feels at this time in the morning. When the sun is only just coming up and the birds are singing. He can walk around the garden and enjoy the feeling of stillness it holds. He felt privileged to be one of the few people who could enjoy the garden when no one else was around. Even during heavy rain, there would still be people taking strolls through the garden, many of them appreciating how the garden seemed that little bit happier whenever there was a downpour.

He always appreciated the feeling of the cobbles under his feet. In the Summer months he would take advantage of the earlier morning sun by heading to the garden even earlier in the morning. When he had finished his jobs, he would remove his shoes and walk on the cool cobbles in his bare feet. If it had been an uncomfortably hot night, the feeling of the cobbles on his feet would be a pleasant relief.

Peter then headed to the large oak tree at the back of the garden. This was the largest tree in the garden and Peter would go and sit under it for a few minutes every morning. It was just a place where he could have five minutes to himself and enjoy the peaceful nature of the garden. He would sit cross legged and just look at the tree. Just taking in how impressive and beautiful it was. How for many it was the highlight of the garden. He would sit and watch the morning sunlight bursting through the few gaps in the branches.

He thought about the day this tree was planted. He was around eight years old and his father wanted to make improvements to the rear of the garden. Peter asked his dad if he could plant his own oak tree, the first thing he would ever plant. His father helped him prepare the earth and did the hole while Peter planted the seeds. His father then piled earth onto the seeds and made it even. Peter couldn't wait to see how big the tree would become.

When they left the garden that morning, Peter's father gave him a penny and told him to make a wish in the fountain. Peter held the coin tightly, closed his eyes and concentrated on his wish. He wanted it to come true more than anything and he knew that the garden could make it happen if he just believed. He then took in a deep breath and threw the coin into the fountain. He opened his eyes and watched the coin sink slowly down to the bottom of the fountain. When his father asked him what he wished for, Peter said he couldn't say because then it wouldn't come true. His father smiled and told him that as long as he kept his wish secret, the garden may well make the wish come true.

On this beautiful morning, Peter smiled at the memory of his father. He looked up at the beautiful oak tree and thought about how in that moment, the garden really had been magic. Peter took one last look at the oak tree. The largest tree in the garden and his pride and joy.

He then took his gardening equipment and started to leave the garden, leaving it ready for the day ahead. Peter wondered what other wishes would be made in the Magic Garden today and if any of them would become true. After all, Peter knew that if you wished hard enough, the garden really would be magic.

8. Picnic Near the Waterfall (50 Minutes)

Hello and welcome to tonight's sleep story for adults. Before we begin, make sure that you are nice and comfortable in bed. Get nice and warm under the covers. Stretch out if you can and enjoy the space you have around you. Take a moment to fully settle into a comfortable position. Become more aware of the bed supporting your body. Enjoy the feeling of the pillow gently supporting your head. Then, when you are happy, take in a nice deep breath. Hold it inside for a moment and then exhale slowly. Now gently close your eyes and allow your mind to power down. Know that this is the time to settle down and rest. End any thoughts you might be having. Just gently allow your mind to clear as you get ready for the picnic near the waterfall.

As you walk through the dense woodland towards the waterfall, you feel a great sense of excitement. You can't wait to get to the waterfall and settle down with the picnic basket you are carrying with you. For the last few days, it feels like it has been raining constantly. Every time you have looked out of your window and thought about how much you have wanted to go for a picnic, you have been repelled by the sight of dense, grey and dark clouds hanging above you. They have been sending down a hammering of rain for what feels like an eternity.

This morning however, things are different. You have awoken to the sight of a beautiful blue sky. The only clouds you have seen are thin and wispy and certainly pose no threat to the warm and inviting climate. You can tell it must have been warm overnight as the ground is completely dry. Even the grass just outside your home feels comfortable. Certainly comfortable enough to sit and lie back on, especially if you have a soft blanket helping to support you.

As soon as you saw the sky this morning, you knew that you could not waste this opportunity. You packed up your picnic basket. You filled it with your favourite sandwiches and snacks and a flask filled with tea. You grabbed a blanket and stuffed it into the basket and then ran out of the door. The state of euphoria you feel almost makes you forget to lock your door as you leave the house and head towards the woodland about half a mile from your home.

Now, you are walking through that woodland. With each step that you take, you are moving closer and closer to the waterfall. You can hear the crashing water already even though you know you still have a little further to walk. In this woodland, you can't hear any of the traffic on the motorway in the distance. You can just about see some of the cars through the gaps in the trees but the gentle humming of their engines can't seem to penetrate the trees. It's almost like the soundwaves know they would be unwelcome in this place. This is a place of tranquility and calmness. A place where people can visit and feel one with nature. A place where they can come and leave all of the worries and pressures of modern life at home.

With every step you are taking through the woodland, you can feel yourself becoming more and more relaxed. All of those things that have been bothering you or making you feel stressed in life have been left behind. You closed the door on them as soon as you left the house with your picnic basket. Right now, all you have to do is relax and enjoy your surroundings. Enjoy being in the here and now. Enjoy the woodland and wonderful sounds that nature provides. The sound of the breeze gently flowing through the gaps in the tree branches. The sound of distant birds. Some of them move closer as they sing, hopping along from tree to tree around you. The sound of their chirping almost sounds like they are greeting you to the woodland.

You can almost feel the vibrations of the waterfall in the ground now. In your mind, you can see the crashing waves as you move ever closer. The vibrations caused by the crashing water feel like they are moving through your body. It almost feels like you are being given a gentle massage. Like the waterfall is already trying to ease any feelings of tension out of your body. Any feelings of tension you might have been holding in your back or in your shoulders or neck are slowly being soothed by the vibrations. And with each step towards the waterfall you take, you can feel the vibrations getting stronger.

You enjoy the smell of the pine trees around you. As you walk, you can see small beads of water dripping down from the branches onto the dry forest floor below them. These last remnants of the rainfall are now slowly drying away. You can almost hear the small drops as they come down from the high branches, hitching rides on the branches further down until eventually they are able to gracefully make the short drop down to the gravelly ground.

Finally, as you notice the trees starting to become increasingly less dense, you emerge out into the clearing. And there in front of you is the top of the waterfall. You take a moment to fully appreciate how beautiful it looks. How comforting it is to hear the sound of the water crashing down below you. As you look down, you see the steam from the water as it impacts the stream below, before the water calms and forms a gentle lake the sweeps off into the distance.

Just by standing here, you can feel tension that you could have been holding inside of you for years slowly starting to drift away. You remember why you have come to this place and why you have been so eager to come here. This place is the home of total tranquillity. This is a place where all worries and troubles can be washed away, almost like they are being released over the edge of the waterfall. Just being allowed to slip away on the delicate stream below.

You take the blanket out of your picnic basket and gently lay it down on the grass. You sit down on the blanket and place your basket beside you. You take a moment to simply look out onto the waterfall. You can still hear the birds singing around you. You can even spot one or two of them flying gracefully over the edge of the waterfall as they move to the collection of dense trees on the opposite side of where you are sitting.

Fully take in how wonderful it feels to be here. Now lie back on your blanket so you are looking up at the clear sky. You can still see some of the dense trees swaying in the gentle breeze in the corner of your eye. You watch the few thin clouds above you move through the sky. You enjoy the feeling of the warm sun on your skin. It doesn't feel too hot. It's just right. Just enough to make you feel comfortable and to compliment the breeze perfectly.

Now, as you listen to the sound of the crashing waterfall just a few steps away from you, gently allow your eyes to close. Feel the breeze and the sunshine. Listen to the distant birds and the sound of the crashing waterfall as you slowly drift off to sleep. All the while, still fully experiencing how wonderful it is to have this time to lie back and fully enjoy the magical wonder of this gracious and breathtaking waterfall.

9. A Night On Your Paradise Island (70 Minutes)

Hello and welcome to tonight's sleep story. Tonight, we will be spending the night on your own personal paradise island. This is a place that belongs to you and you alone. So, take a moment to get nice and comfortable. Allow your mind to slow down and you get comfortable in bed. Get into a position where you feel like you could fall asleep and then allow your eyes to close. Take in a few deep breaths and then slowly release the air. Do this a few times until you notice any tension that you may be holding slowly leaving your body. Then when you feel completely comfortable, allow yourself to breathe at a normal pace. Now that you are ready and you are completely comfortable in bed, we can travel to your paradise island.

As you stand on the beach at Paradise Island, you watch the sun as it starts to set over the horizon. A blushing colour of orange and yellow bursting in the distance. Watching the ebb and flow of the waves as they gently crash against the sea, try and make your breath line up with the waves. Breathing in deeply as the water hits the shore and then breathing out as the waves retreat back into the vast ocean. Watch the waves come in and pull back again.

You appreciate the feeling of the gentle breeze as it flows around you. You take in a deep breath and savour the feeling of the sea air entering your airways. Above you, you can see the beautiful sky. It's filled with an array of colours as the day begins the transition to night. You look at the sky turning to a lighter shade of blue in the distance, where the sky is meeting the lowering sun over the distant horizon. You enjoy the feeling of the sand underneath your bare feet. You feel an amazing sense of connection with the island and indeed the world around you.

There is no one around you. No one for miles around. This is almost your own personal place. A private oasis where you can feel connected with the earth. A place to feel one with the planet and with the natural world. Away from bustling cities or a hectic workplace. Nothing but you and your surroundings.

You watch as the sun continues to set over the horizon. After a few moments, it gets replaced by the bright moon as it rises in the sky. You notice the reflection its casting into the sea, like a silver orb of light and energy. As the waves move, it's almost like the reflection is dancing on the surface of the water. You watch as stars start to come out to play for night.

Soon they're filling the sky. There are so many colours. From purple to a lighter blue to a much heavier, darker blue. The moon and stars illuminate the beach. You're surrounded by their natural light as you listen to the waves continue to gently wash against the beach.

You take in a deep breath. You feel more and more relaxed in these surroundings. Your connection with Paradise Island is making you feel more happy. As a reaction, your entire body starts to relax. The muscles in your head and your face. Your jaw starts to loosen. Any tension in your chest and stomach just drifting away. All the muscles in your arms and your legs become heavy and relaxing. The only thing you are aware of now are your feet. Your feet as they connect you to the sandy beach. As they connect you to the earth and the pure nature around you.

You take a moment to simply observe your breathing. Notice the warm sea air filling your lungs. And then as you breath out, the sea carries away any tension or stress you may be feeling. Once again you try and match your breathing with the movement of the waves. You take in a nice deep breath as the waves hit the sandy beach. And then you breathe out as the water slowly retreats back into the vast ocean. While you're doing this, you continue to take in the beauty of the stars and the moon. You watch as their light dances on the surface of the ocean. They're illuminating the night with their calming energy.

You turn around and take in the rest of the island. All you can hear is the soft waves hitting the beach as you watch the palm trees. They are blowing gently in the cool sea breeze, almost like a gentle swaying. As you walk further into the island, you start to notice the sound of crickets as well, almost joining the waves and the breeze in a chorus of songs.

You notice how the palm trees all look so strong and stable. You touch one of them as you walk past and you can almost feel the energy from the tree being passed into your body. A calming energy that is making you feel more relaxed.

You feel completely safe as you walk deeper into the island. You feel like nothing can disturb you during this moment. You are experiencing pure calmness and relaxation. During this moment of oneness, you feel completely connected with the world around you. And you have been able to find this wonderful feeling through the power of your own mind. This is your personal place. No one can disturb you here.

Stop walking for a moment and sit down on the ground. You cross your legs and sit with your back resting against the tree. You look up at the stars and you feel like this is the first time you have really seen the stars. The first time you have really taken in how far away there are. How vast the universe is and what a gift it is to be a living being in the middle of the miracle of creation.

The sounds of crickets and birds join in to form a chorus with the sound of the waves. You enjoy listening to these sounds as they fill the night air. You take in another deep, relaxing breath and fill your lungs with sea air. As you breathe out, you release those last bits of tension in your body as you get back to your feet and continue walking deeper towards the heart of the island.

You feel fully present while you are here. Like you only exist in this current moment and nothing else matters. You feel a warmth inside you and a happiness. And you know that really, this is how you should feel most of the time. This is how human beings should feel. They should feel calm and appreciative of the world around them. And they should be able to fully enjoy moments like this.

As you move through the trees, you come to a lovely, tranquil pond. You take a moment then you decide to climb into the pond. You enjoy the feeling of the cool and comforting water as it washes over your skin.

Even the nights are quite warm on your paradise island, so having this place to cool down feels very welcome. You enjoy the feeling of the water on your skin as you move deeper into the water. You keep moving until nearly your entire body is submerged. You take a moment to fully enjoy the cool sensations washing over you. It's almost like you are being held by a nice thin blanket as you settle down to enjoy the warm evenings that this personal paradise has to offer.

You kick your legs back and allow yourself to start floating on the surface of the pond. All you can see above you is the night sky as you start drifting down the pond. You enjoy the feeling of weightlessness. It's almost like you are a feather floating on a gentle breeze.

You continue to float down the pond now as you look up again to the night sky. You take in the beauty of it as the crickets and the birds continue with their evening songs. As you float further and further down the pond, the sound of the waves become more and more distant.

You enjoy the embrace of the water. You feel like you can let go of everything you have been holding on to. You let go of any stresses or worries. You let go of any bad feelings you have about others or yourself. You let it all go as it all sinks to the bottom of the pond while you continue to float.

As you reach the edge of the lake, you climb onto the side and lie down. You continue looking up at the night sky as you allow the warm air to slowly dry your skin. You can still feel the cool feelings of the water settling into your skin. Sinking deeper even to your muscles. You close your eyes and enjoy the feelings moving slowly through your body right now. All you can hear now is the sound of the birds and crickets as they serenade you through the night as you slowly drift off to a relaxing and rejuvenating sleep.

10. A Trip Down the River (60 Minutes)

Hello and welcome to tonight's sleep story. Tonight, we are going to go on a nice calming trip down the river. But before we do, it's important that we are nice and comfortable for the journey. So, get nice and comfortable under the covers. When you are ready, close your eyes and just allow the bed to support your body. Allow your head to sink into the pillow. Just allow your body to rest and begin the process of recharging. Take in some deep breaths and then allow the air to slowly leave your body. Imagine that the air you are breathing out is carrying any tension that you feel you might be holding in your muscles. Then, once you have done this a few times, simply breathe normally. Now, we will begin our journey.

The river is always an amazing place to visit at night. Many people say that this river in particular is good to visit. Many say that if you go during the daylight hours, you're not going to get the full effect of the river and the life that inhabits along its banks until you go at night. It's then that the river truly comes to life and you can fully experience what it has to offer.

The flowers along the banks all look calm and content. The sunflowers are all huddled together, almost like the are snuggling up for a comfortable night's sleep. Other flowers around all have thick, green stalks, like they are braced for any sort of change in the elements over the course of time. Just by looking at them, you can see that they have been around for a while and that they are prepared for anything. It would take more than a strong wind or a heavy downpour of rain and hail to break their spirits. Even if you were stood their in the worst of snowstorms, these flowers would still all be standing defiantly tall. Undisturbed by the elements as they carried on with their lives.

As you walk along the bank, you notice that some of the other flowers are moving more strongly in the breeze. As you listen to the trickle of the water as it moves down the river, you wonder if the flowers are actually dancing in response to the rhythmic sounds. Some of the sunflowers along the side are drooping their heads lower, almost like they are trying to reach down and take a sip from the flowing water.

As you continue walking, you notice a thick tree trunk that has fallen into the river. It's clearly been there for some time. For many places, the sight of a fallen tree would be a bad thing. But here, the river has seen an opportunity to make something beautiful.

Over the years, the river has helped make the tree trunk part of the impressive scenery. Moss has started to grow over the trunk to form a comfortable green carpet. You notice a couple of frogs have jumped onto the log and seem to be enjoying the comfort of the moss under their webbed feet. It's admirable how this place has even been able to take something like the death of a tree and turn it into an opportunity to create a unique characteristic for itself. Something that the animals and plants alike on this river will be able to experience and enjoy.

As you continue to walk, you can see more of the trees in the distance. As you look further ahead, you can see where the river slopes off into the dense woodland. Even though you are far away from this part of the river, you can still hear the animals that live along its banks. The birds are finishing their days of singing and are beginning to settle down for the night. You can also hear the owls that are hooting good morning to the river as they get ready to start their night.

On the opposite side of the river, you can see the apple trees along the banks. During the summer months, children frequently come here and pick the apples from the trees. Anyone who has ever eaten an apple from one of these trees says that they are the best they have ever tasted and that it's the air and the quality of the soil around the river that give the apples such an amazing flavour. Right now, there are a collection of green and red apples hanging invitingly down from the branches. Some of them seem quite low down to the floor, almost like the trees are mindful of small children who might not be able to reach some of the apples on the higher branches.

As you look above, you can see the stars and the moon have finally come out to begin their evenings. When they come into view, they illuminate your path. The moon shimmers down on the river, almost like a spotlight. And when it does, you can see some of the fish still swimming around beneath the surface. You can see only a couple of first, but then you see a large group travelling upstream together. You watch them as they delicately sway against the current. They're not moving very fast, but then again, nothing needs to move fast in this place. By this river, time can simply come to stop and everything is okay.

As you start to think about how magical it would be to bring a boat down this river and sit on the deck, drinking tea from a flask and wrapped in a warm blanket, you can feel any stresses or worries you may have been having slowly drifting away. That is how powerful this river can be. Here, there is no need to feel stress. There is nothing commanding your immediate attention. All you have to do is relax and become one with the nature and wonderful life around you.

You continue thinking about how wonderful it would be to take a boat down here. How you could take pictures of all the plants and animals as you float by. You could get a closer look at the frogs that were on the fallen tree. You know that they would not be spooked by your presence. You can tell that they would be more than happy to see you and would feel comfortable with you around.

You see some stepping stones over a more shallow part of the river. You use them to get to the other side and when you do, you decide you must know about the truth about those apples. You decide to pick a red one from one of the branches. It shines like a jewel and you can almost see the reflection of the stars on its skin. You take one bite and as you do, you can already tell that those people were right all along. It's so juicy and full of flavour. As you swallow your mouthful, it almost feels like the apple is making your body feel more relaxed and calm. You take another bite and you notice that your muscles are releasing their tension. Some of the tension you are releasing feels like something that you have been holding inside of yourself for a long time. It feels wonderful to finally be able to let it go. Almost like you have thrown it into the river and are now watching it slowly float away.

You take a moment to just simply stand and listen to the sound of the wind flowing through the trees. Along with the sound of the owls and the movement of the river, it feels like you're being serenaded. And as the crickets start to join in for a peaceful chorus, you allow yourself to drift off to sleep. Have a nice peaceful sleep now, knowing that you can come back and have another trip down the river whenever you want.

www.ingramcontent.com/pod-product-compliance
Lightning Source LLC
Chambersburg PA
CBHW062158100526
44589CB00014B/1869